Presented To

_____

From

_____

Date

_____

Breaking Out of Your Prison

Breaking Out of Your Prison

12 Keys that Unlock the Door

Ray Kauffman

Copyright 2013 – Ray L. Kauffman

All rights reserved. This book is protected by the copyright laws of the United States of America. This book may not be copied or reprinted for commercial gain or profit. The use of short quotations or occasional page copying for personal use is permitted and encouraged. Permission will be granted upon request.
Unless otherwise identified, Scripture quotations are from the New King James Version. Copyright © 1982 by Thomas Nelson, Inc. Used by permission. All rights reserved. Scripture quotations marked NIV are from THE HOLY BIBLE, NEW INTERNATIONAL VERSION®, NIV® Copyright © 1973, 1978, 1984, 2011 by Biblica, Inc.™ Used by permission. All rights reserved worldwide.

Ray L. Kauffman
395 Lincoln Way East
Chambersburg PA 17201

ISBN 13: 978-0-9892680-0-4

For Worldwide Distribution, Printed in the United States.

1 2 3 4 5 6 7 / 16 15 14 13

ENDORSEMENTS

Ray has written a great book for inmates, their family and loved ones. It is wonderful for individual and group counseling on the effects of doing time and the stressful emotions we go through. I was released from prison in 1987 and have worked with troubled youth for 25 years.

Dana Gonzales

The concepts and language identifying emotions were clear and easily understood. In my own jail chaplaincy ministry, many inmates have had to deal with the range of emotions identified by the author. Questions for further reflection are helpful for those using this book as a resource to help people along their journey to acceptance and change.

Isaac Burkholder, Chaplain FCJ

DEDICATION

This book is dedicated to the three most important women in my life. They are my wife, Georgia, and my daughters, Michelle and Angela. Their love, support, and encouragement during my preparation for ministry and throughout the years have been heartwarming and appreciated. They continue to be my most valuable assets and are loved and appreciated more every day.

ACKNOWLEDGMENTS

It is important the reader knows why this book was dedicated to my family. For me, ministry was a second career. When God called me to Christian ministry I was married with two daughters. I left a career in the postal service, enrolled in college, and then went on to seminary. Not only that, but I was assigned to a medium-size rural United Methodist Church as a student pastor. To say the least, my family and I had a hectic schedule.

During that time until the present, I have been blessed by many others who have been part of the ministry in numerous and various ways. During my last year in college an internship was required, and I thank the local mental health, mental retardation unit and the prison warden who were instrumental in starting a part-time internship at our local prison. It was from this meager beginning the full-time chaplaincy at Franklin County Prison began and continues to this day.

This experience whetted my appetite to return to full-time prison ministry after completing seminary and ordination. I thank St. John's United Methodist Church in Chambersburg,

Pennsylvania, for the seven years I had the opportunity to serve as their pastor and for their spiritual care, nurture, and support during those learning years. I am grateful to the churches of our local community who then and now largely support the local prison ministry.

A great deal of gratitude goes to the Central Pennsylvania (now Susquehanna) Conference of the United Methodist Church that, through the extension ministry program, endorsed my serving in prison chaplaincy.

Last but not least I want to thank a dear friend and mentor, Dean Drawbaugh. Without his friendship, guidance, and support, this book would not be possible.

Thanks to everyone whose love and support has been and continues to be priceless in my spiritual journey.

CONTENT

Foreword 15

Introduction 17

Key 1 Dealing with Anxieties 21

Key 2 Dealing with Denial 29

Key 3 Dealing with Authority 35

Key 4 Dealing with Anger........................41

Key 5 Dealing with Loneliness 49

Key 6 Dealing with Plea-Bargaining...............57

Key 7 Dealing with Fears 65

Key 8 Dealing with Depression...................71

Key 9 Dealing with Reality 77

Breaking Out of Your Prison

Key 10 Dealing with Acceptance............................85

Key 11 Dealing with Temptation.............................91

Key 12 Dealing with the Future..............................99

Conclusion...107

FOREWORD

One of my favorite books is *As a Man Thinketh* by James Allen. Applying its lessons to this book you are holding, author Allen might relate, "When you act like a prisoner you will become a prisoner. When you stop acting like a prisoner you will free yourself from your prison." It takes only a few sentences to describe most wisdom but sometimes a lifetime to master.

A quick look at the chapter titles in this book reveals a laundry list of emotions that hold each of us back: anxieties, denial, authority, anger, loneliness, plea bargaining, fears, depression, reality, acceptance, temptation, and hope for the future. Reviewing my life, I faced these emotions at every crossroad. It is easy to see how a few wrong choices could have made me a prisoner.

In this book, Ray Kauffman effectively ties a prisoner's emotions to the actions that cause people to be imprisoned and are keeping them in prison. More importantly, Ray creates the blueprint to move each of us from a prisoner mentality to a freedom mentality. He shares a plan to drive the negative

Breaking Out of Your Prison

emotions out of our minds and create space for the positive emotions: love, joy, peace, patience, kindness, goodness, faithfulness, gentleness, and self-control. Against such things there is no law and no need for prisons (see Galatians 5:22-23).

Ray *believes* these principles, *practices* these principles, and *lives* these principles. His faith allows him to walk into the "lions den" daily and make a difference in the lives of "prisoners" such as you and me. It is my wish that each reader of this book will pay it forward by sharing this timeless message with those who need it.

Dean Drawbaugh

Introduction

Breaking Out of Your Prison

While this book is written for the prisoner, it may be helpful for anyone who is dealing with a crisis situation. For in difficult situations we can all let our emotions get out of control. An event such as the sudden death of a loved one, an unexpected illness, a relationship gone badly, or an imprisonment in a correctional institution can test our emotions. It is even possible that strong emotions like revenge, fear, hate, etc. can imprison us within ourselves.

We are emotional, physical, mental, and spiritual beings. We are creatures of emotions. All emotions are not bad; it is only when they get out of control that they can adversely affect us, including family, friends, prison staff, volunteers, or visitors. We know that when a family member or friend is in any crisis, we are affected in some way. It is my hope that anyone dealing with irrational emotions of incarceration or other crisis will find this book helpful.

Breaking Out of Your Prison

The focus of this book is the prisoners, to help guide them through their prison experience. It can also be used for group settings and discussion.

Anyone who has been in prison or visited a loved one there knows firsthand the emotions associated with doing time in prison. In fact I have heard many times how even the visitors feel like prisoners for various reasons. Imprisonment separates families and is expensive to the taxpayer at all levels of government. In our local county in rural south central Pennsylvania, 75 percent of tax dollars are budgeted for the criminal justice system.

The U.S. Bureau of Justice Statistics in 2011 reported that 6,977,700 people were either incarcerated in federal, state, and local prisons or on probation or parole. This does not include 70,792 juveniles in detention centers in 2009. It is estimated that about 2.9 percent of the U.S. population is either in prison or on probation or parole.

It has also been reported that a college education is less expensive than keeping a prisoner, which is in most cases exceeds $40,000 a year. Hopefully you can see why and how getting emotions under control can only make for better families and communities. Controlling emotions cannot only help the one in prison but can also keep the person from returning. May this be our collective goal!

In these writings you will find quotes from some well known and from some not so well known people. There are also

Breaking Out of Your Prison

references from the Bible. All of these quotes are from people who have lived before us and from whom we can all learn.

During my college and seminary days, the one thing I learned above all else was how much I didn't know. As I grow older, that realization hasn't changed. I continue to be amazed at how much I don't know and how the scriptures can provide insightful tips for everyday living. That is true whether you believe in God or not. So it is my hope and prayer that you may find constructive ways to deal with your emotions—in or out of prison.

Key 1

Dealing with Anxieties

…you do not know what a day may bring forth
(Proverbs 27:1).

"Why am I here? What did I do to deserve this? Can I make a phone call? Can I see my wife? Can I call my attorney? Can I call my parole officer? When can I have a visit? When can I have my medications?" These are questions asked by almost everyone as they are brought into prison. I have heard them many times as a prison chaplain.

These questions and other concerns can cause many anxieties and anxious moments. Yes, a day, an hour, or even a minute can change our circumstances drastically. From childhood to death no one escapes disappointment, sickness, death, loss of a meaningful relationship, crisis, and difficulty of some sort.

So if we experience many of these circumstances, why do some people deal with them better than others? Why does it

Breaking Out of Your Prison

seem like some people are always dealing with problems and others are breezing along in life seemingly problem-free? For those with many problems, if you ask them how they are doing you may be in for an earful.

Anxiety and being anxious are caused by anything that makes us feel that we have lost control. While some of our life problems may be self-inflicted, many are not. We can't always control sickness or prevent accidents. We can be in the wrong place at the wrong time. Often the economic climate and technology affect our employment status. Many times we have to retrain and start over.

A major change in a meaningful relationship, a sudden illness or injury, or the loss of a loved one can throw us a real challenge. Sometimes life choices or bad habits can cause pain as well.

Years ago I was visiting an elderly friend in the hospital who was suffering from emphysema caused by many years of smoking. He had been advised by his doctor and others many times to stop, but he didn't. He said to me, "Ray, if I had listened to good advice, I wouldn't be here grasping for my breath. This is a horrible way to die."

It is interesting how we often learn the hard way rather than learn from others' mistakes. A song made popular many years ago by Frank Sinatra says it well, "I'll do it my way"—often to find out it was the wrong way.

Dealing with Anxieties

We never know at the beginning of each day if we may end up in a doctor's office, the hospital, or prison. As we plan a normal day, these places are usually not on our schedule, unless we have an appointment.

***

How we handle our day-to-day experiences can stir many emotions. We enjoy days of laughter, time with family and friends, or using our skills and abilities to provide a living for family or ourselves. These activities bring us feelings of love, acceptance, and fulfillment.

On the other hand, if we experience the loss of a job, an unexpected illness, death, or a break in a long time relationship, we can experience emotions of loneliness, frustration, anger, and depression to name only a few. These are the emotions that often lead to actions that not only hurt us but others too.

These are the emotions that cause people to do things that entangle them with the law. When emotions get out of control, it may take others to manage us. Prison can be the result.

Have you ever said, "I'll never do that," "That will never happen to me," or "I'll never get caught"? Have you ever broken the speed limit or other traffic laws? Have you ever used the company's office supplies for your personal use? Have you ever wasted time or spent time doing personal things at work on

Breaking Out of Your Prison

your boss's time clock? If your employment involves the use of a computer, it is so easy to use it for personal use. We often hear of employees dismissed from their employment for the unlawful use of equipment or services. I'm sure they thought they would "never get caught."

However small the infraction may be, we are all guilty, aren't we? Now I am not trying to put you on a guilt trip. But it is easy to judge others, while we have our own faults to face or correct. No matter what the "crime," we create our own prison within ourselves if we don't take responsibility for it and make it right.

I had an interesting conversation once with a dear friend, a banker. We met periodically for breakfast, sharing support and exchange of ideas. One morning we were on the subject of why people do the things they do. I said to him, "Suppose we were both driving down the highway speeding, and you got caught and I didn't, which one of us was wrong?" The obvious answer is we both were because we were both exceeding the speed limit, but one got caught and the other didn't, one had to pay a fine and the other didn't. Depending on how much over the speed limit he was driving, he may even get "points" placed on his driving record.

I continued, "So which one of us would feel the best about our experience? I would be glad I didn't get caught. But you may say, 'Yeah, I got caught, but you were just as guilty as I

Dealing with Anxieties

was because you were breaking the law too.'" True? I think he got the point.

Do you know that not even the U.S. Justice Department can tell us how many federal, state, and local laws there are? It is estimated to be in the millions. From 2000-2007 Congress created 452 new federal offenses. The total number of federal laws at the end of 2007 totaled 4,500. So it would be difficult to believe there would be anyone who has not broken a law knowingly or unknowingly. The book of James in Bible says, *"For whoever shall keep the whole law, and yet stumble in one point, he is guilty of all"* (James 2:10).

It is interesting to consider God gave Moses ten laws to live by. Jesus reduced that to two: to love God and your neighbor; and we can't even keep two!

As we have often heard, everyone makes mistakes. So one of the first things as a prisoner and as a loved one of a prisoner is to realize our own human nature. You may have heard the expression, "There, but for the grace of God, go I." Yes, you may be the one caught, but throwing yourself a pity party will not help you. Rather, own your mistake and learn from it.

I don't intend to compare a traffic ticket with more serious offenses. I know few go to prison because of a traffic violation, unless another person may have been killed or injured in a traffic accident because of speeding or DUI. Whatever the

Breaking Out of Your Prison

reason for being incarcerated, it can be a learning and growing experience. You and those you love will both benefit if you choose to keep a positive attitude and know that you can make it right.

***

So how do we handle all the emotions we experience? Emotions are part of our personality and we have to deal with them in some way. How we handle them can make or break our day and our life. It is true that "it is not what happens to us but how we handle what happens to us" that makes the difference in our lives.

So how will you deal with your emotions today? Hopefully this book will help you deal positively with your emotions—your anxieties.

Whatever comes your way today, take time to ask yourself: Is this something I can do anything about? Do I have any control over the situation? Is it a result of a decision I made? Did I do anything to contribute to the situation? If you didn't, then move on and make it a great day—enjoy it. But if it happened because of a bad habit, your lifestyle, or your friends, then you must decide what you can do to correct the situation.

Three questions I ask myself when I am about to make a decision are:

Dealing with Anxieties

1. Will it be good for me?
2. Will it be good for another person?
3. Will it be good for society?

If you can answer yes to those three questions, then continue cautiously. So how are you doing so far?

Breaking Out of Your Prison

Points to Ponder

STOP! Before you deal with the next Key reflect on the following questions:

1. When have you felt anxiety?

2. What caused you anxiety?

3. If this situation happened again, how would you handle it?

Key 2

Dealing with Denial

It's not denial, I'm just selective about the reality I accept.
—Bill Watterson

I can still remember when I was contacted about my nephew who was killed in an auto accident by a drunk driver. It was my wife, a dear friend, and I who had to break the news to my brother and his wife.

I remember when my doctor told me I had cancer and surgery was necessary.

I remember when I was told I needed open heart surgery.

None of these circumstances were expected. In fact, I felt fine and had no symptoms of either my cancer or heart problems. My first response to all of these unexpected realities was shock. I did not want to believe any of them. Being told you have to have surgery when you don't feel sick, rates close to

Breaking Out of Your Prison

being told you are going to prison, regardless of the reason. I am grateful that my cancer and heart surgeries were successful, and I experience relative good health to this day.

One of our first reactions when something unexpected happens to us is, "I can't believe it." It is difficult to hear bad news, and going to prison is one of them.

In the book *On Death and Dying,* Dr. Elizabeth Kubler-Ross writes about the five stages of dying. She named them as denial, anger, bargaining, depression, and acceptance. Those stages have been applied to many situations in life. They certainly apply to the prison experience.

From my personal experiences, I have added a few to Dr. Ross's five stages that add more light to the emotions of what the incarcerated and their loved ones feel. By incarcerated I mean not only those behind physical bars within a physical prison building, but also those who are behind emotional bars within the prison they have built inside themselves.

Let's consider the first one: *denial.* If you know you are going to prison or are in prison, the first reaction is, "I can't believe this is happening to me. This can't be real." Whether it is expected or happens in the blink of an eye, human nature is to disbelieve something traumatic is happening. "This is interrupting my schedule, work, family, social life…this is anything but pleasant." We are in denial.

Dealing with Denial

So how do you handle the fact that it really *is* real? It isn't a dream or nightmare? You really *are* facing a crisis. How do you deal with it? The big question is: how did you actually get to this point of imprisonment?

One of the statements I heard often after asking this question was, "I thought I could beat the charges." Then I would ask, "What do you mean by that? Do you mean you did not do the crime, or that it can't be proven?" The usual answer was "*They* can't prove it." *They* mean the law community.

Anyone who has faced the criminal justice system knows that often times multiple charges are filed against the accused. So as we would talk about the charges and situation, my suggestion was whatever the charges the person was guilty of, confess and deal with them.

Naturally my suggestion was not wholeheartedly accepted.

You may try to beat the charges, pass blame on someone else, or just simply deny them, but sooner or later the deceit will catch up with you—and in the meantime, you will only cause yourself more anxiety.

Also consider the first time someone becomes involved with the courts the person is often not charged with a serious felony only a misdemeanor. So if the person owns his or her mistake and learns from it right away, the person may save years of frustration for himself and his loved ones.

Breaking Out of Your Prison

You may say but it isn't easy to confess to something that all my friends are doing and they didn't get caught. Why me? That is not your problem. Their time may be coming. Right now you have to deal with *your* situation. Remember being in prison not only affects you, but family and loved ones as well.

One time in a chapel service I asked those present to hold up a finger for each person affected by them being in prison. The average was seven people. You are not the only one who suffers when you do something that lands you in prison.

We live in a self-centered society—all that matters is my feelings, my wants, my desires, and too often we don't consider other persons' feelings and desires. If you want to help yourself, be true and honest with yourself. If you want to do your time and get on with your life, it is necessary to face those situations and emotions that will make your time in prison more bearable and prevent you from coming back, again, and again.

If you have any goal while in prison it should be to ask yourself every day, "What do I need to learn from this experience that will prevent me from coming back." I have met few people who want to repeat their prison experience. If you don't want to return, then it requires making changes in how you deal with the temptations and challenges of daily living. Remember the saying, "You can't do the same things over and over and expect to get different results."

Dealing with Denial

If you are released from prison and have not dealt honestly with your emotions, you can expect to return to prison. It is that simple. Is that what you really want?

Let me conclude this section with a similar question asked before:

1. Are the decisions you are making good for you now and in the future?
2. Will your decisions be best for someone you love for now and the future?
3. Will your choices be good for society for now and the future?

Breaking Out of Your Prison

Points to Ponder

STOP! Before you deal with the next Key reflect on the following questions:

1. When have you felt denial?

2. What is the reason for your denial?

3. How can you deal with the denial?

Key 3

Dealing with Authority

Football is like life—it requires perseverance, self-denial, hard work, sacrifice, dedication and respect for authority.
—Vince Lombardi

"I am so tired of everyone telling me what to do. The guards tell me when I can eat, when I can shower, when I can exercise, when I can make a phone call, when I go to bed, when the lights go out. They tell me if or when I get a visit. I am tired of it," said an inmate.

I have heard many inmates expressing these same frustrations. I left out a couple of expletives.

"Welcome" is not a word you will hear as you enter prison, nor is it a word you want to hear. No one looks forward to going to prison, even less so than anyone looks forward to going to the hospital.

Breaking Out of Your Prison

The one thing that causes anxieties in prison is knowing you are not in charge of yourself. From the moment you enter until you walk out your every move is at someone else's discretion. Even volunteers and visitors don't move from one place to another unless a correctional officer or staff opens the electronic doors. Some staff members even have limited control or access to certain areas of the prison.

So if you have trouble with authority, it won't be easy to live inside a prison and accept orders from those in charge, whether in a cinderblock prison or a flesh and blood prison.

Authority is one thing that you will not only want to deny or argue about but it will make you angry, maybe downright mad. You learn quickly you will be told when to do everything. Your every move is under someone else's control and discretion. You are not in charge—of anything. That is not acceptable to our human nature. We as individuals like to be in charge. We want to do what we want, when we want, where we want, and how we want.

Another inmate wrote on the front of a church program: "Authority is a person who has the power or right over us, from God to Guards, surrender!" This inmate "got it"—he realized there is a point when a person has to submit to authority.

To fight against the system only causes yourself a lot more anxiety and frustration. The earlier you recognize and respect prison authorities, the better you will get along with staff and other inmates.

Dealing with Authority

Remember, prison is not your home, unless you are sentenced for life. In either case, debating policies, procedures, and schedules will not earn you much respect from others. To earn respect, you must show respect. I am not saying you should never question anything, but do it in the proper manner, attitude, and channels.

Many prisons have groups and ways of expressing concerns or something you think is unfair. Most of the time I have discovered there is a reason for having the rules they do. It is important to remember that security is the key responsibility of any correctional facility.

If you want to make your prison experience as bearable as possible, obeying the rules and respecting those in charge will go a long way toward accomplishing that goal.

All prisons have ways of dealing with those who buck the rules, disobey, or ignore them. Usually it is in the form of a write-up or disciplinary action with a hearing including the staff member who wrote the report. Many of those hearings result in loss of privileges such as programs, restrictions where you are permitted in the prison, etc.

If you get restricted from eating with other residents, you may even get room (cell) service. Let me tell you, room service may be great in a motel but not in prison. Most inmates want to get out of the cell as much as possible. If you are found guilty of a more serious offense in prison, like fighting, you may be

Breaking Out of Your Prison

confined to your cell, isolation, or "the hole." The hole is just that, a hole (cell) with nothing but limited amenities.

The best way to get along with members of the prison staff is to practice manners. Use words like, "Thank you, Please, May I, I appreciated you listening to me," etc. Call them, Officer Jones, Smith, or whatever name you see on their uniform. Compliment them when appropriate. Try to remember members of the prison staff are human beings too, and you are not the only inmate for which they are responsible. This advice also works for your place of employment, church, and everywhere you deal with people—respect is universal.

***

The Bible says we should pray for those who rule over us (I Timothy 2:1-2) This may be a bold step; but remember, to correct the direction your life is going, you must do something different if you want different results. It is like driving down the highway and discovering you are going the wrong way, if you keep going in the same direction, you are not going to end up at the right place. You need to make a 180-degree turn to reach your destination.

How ready are you to yield to authority? If you have always had difficulty with parents, teachers, a boss at work, or anyone else in authority, then choose to make this an opportunity to learn some new personal skills.

Dealing with Authority

Everyone has some authority over them, and we will never become successful or even content until we learn how to deal with authority.

You don't have to like the person over you, although that helps, but you need to treat the person as a fellow human being. I like what I heard some time ago, "Be kind to everyone you meet today, because everyone is dealing with some kind of a problem." That puts things in perspective. You are not the only one facing a problem or decision. So treat others, no matter who they are, as you want to be treated.

Remember these three questions:

1. Will your words or actions be good for you?
2. Will your words or actions be good for another person?
3. Will your words or actions be good for society?

Can you answer yes to all of these questions? If not, rethink your decision.

Breaking Out of Your Prison

Points to Ponder

STOP! Before dealing with the next Key reflect on the following questions:

1. When do you have a problem with authority?

2. What causes you to question authority?

3. How can you better handle authority?

Key 4

Dealing with Anger

Anger is an acid that can do more harm to the vessel in which it is stored than to anything on which it is poured.
—Mark Twain

The summer following my oldest daughter's graduation from high school, one of her best girlfriends was murdered by her boyfriend in her living room on a warm Sunday afternoon. The question I was asked, "Dad, why and how could anyone do that?" There was no easy or good answer. My response, "That was a terrible tragedy, but yet I have to face him tomorrow with the message that God loves him and offers forgiveness."

Do you think I was angry? Do you think that it was easy for me to face him? Do you think I had emotions boiling inside? Of course I did, who wouldn't?

Back in the 4th century, Greek philosopher Aristotle wrote. "Anyone can become angry—that is easy. But to be angry with the right person and to the right degree and at the right time, and for the right purpose and in the right way—that is not within everyone's power and is not easy."

Everyone feels anger at some time or another. Just living in a world where we see violence, injustice, selfishness, evil, and other symptoms of human nature can cause us anger. The difficulty is knowing how to handle our anger.

Anger is often the second emotion we face when experiencing a crisis. After the initial shock of denial and not wanting to believe what happened, it is very easy to get angry. We can get angry with ourselves, others, or God. Anger is defined as a strong resentment of injury or wrong, wrath, rage, and is often accompanied by the desire to punish. Most people have experienced such situations.

As we learn how to handle anger, it is important to realize that we can feel many emotions at the same time. One feeling can come or go, and we find ourselves dealing with one we have dealt with before.

Too often we tend to think, *I have a right to be angry* when we are frustrated, hurt, attacked, cheated, rejected, and the list goes on. But Jesus tells us to come to terms quickly with our accusers. (see Matthew 5:21-26) The Apostle Paul says, *"Do not let the sun go down on your wrath* [anger]." (Ephesians 4:26). That means we should not go to bed angry, rather we

Dealing with Anger

should quickly make things right with whoever or whatever made us angry.

It has been said that, "He who angers you controls you." I agree. So you have a choice: will anger control you or will you control anger?

Is there an easy way of dealing with your anger? Not always, because often in the heat of the moment you are thinking about yourself, your feelings, your rights, etc. Too often you want revenge on the other person who hurt you or offended you. You often aren't thinking rationally—this is common for most, if not all, people.

***

The best thing to do when you feel yourself getting angry is to walk away or remove yourself from the event or situation. Remember, *it is not always right to do the easy thing and it is not always easy to do the right thing.* This is true whether it is actions or words. How many times have words only made the situation worse? I have often heard, "Engage brain before putting tongue in gear."

Everyone has been hurt by words spoken in anger. Did you know the Bible says, *"Let everyone be quick to listen, slow to speak, slow to anger…The tongue also is a fire, a world of evil among the parts of the body. It corrupts the whole body"* (James 1:19, 3:6 NIV). So harsh words can lead to harmful actions, which often can hurt us more than the other person. So the best, not the easy thing, is to walk away when you begin to feel angry.

What else can you do? Go for a walk. Give yourself time to cool off. Have a cup of coffee. Talk to someone who will listen, a family member or friend. It is not wise to drink alcohol when you're upset. That can only create more problems. Did you know that 70-80 percent of people charged with a crime is the result of alcohol or drugs? Alcohol is often directly or indirectly related to the charge. When people are under the influence of either drugs or alcohol, experts will tell you, it affects their mental ability to process information rationally.

A young female prisoner awaiting sentencing to a state prison and who had problems with alcohol, wrote the following:

> I am so disappointed in myself about the entire situation. I agree with you it may be a blessing in disguise though. My alcoholism was pretty much pushed to the max when my P.O. [probation officer] placed me in here for drinking. I feel like this is the first time I am so determined and sure I want to quit drinking. I think this is the strongest my faith has been as long as I can remember. I just got word that I will be placed in an Intermediate Punishment Program. It will be a long haul. After the state time, I go to an inpatient rehab, then to a half-way house. All in all

Dealing with Anger

though if it is what I need to get better, then I will have to deal with it. I feel like a different person already. Like I have a different outlook. I have been really emotional lately. It is really hard trying to finally deal with all the things and emotions I avoided with alcohol, realizing the things I missed. I have been going to AA every Sunday and that has been helping.

That young lady completed her state time, inpatient rehab and half-way house. She is alcohol free and working.

Everyone has known people who are easy to talk to, kind, and would give you the shirt off their backs; but under the influence of alcohol or drugs they are nasty, rude, and violent. I know several people like that who have spent many years in either local, state, or federal prisons; and each time they return, the charges are more serious. One has gone from drug charges to stealing cars to injuring another person and the last charge was murder. The last charge involved the use of drugs.

It is easy to be critical of others for their actions and think, *Well, that will never happen to me.* But again, if we don't deal with anger in a positive way, it will eventually affect our thinking and our actions. Seek out a pastor or search the book store or Internet for self-help ways to control your anger. Reading the Bible is always the best way to seek answers to life's hardest questions.

***

Breaking Out of Your Prison

A more intense method of overcoming anger is to receive anger management counseling. It can be a suggestion of the courts or mental health staff if an evaluation reveals it may be helpful. Professionals such as a psychiatrist or psychologist are equipped for this type of counseling. While this may be a more costly way of dealing with your anger, it is not too expensive if it helps you get a grip on your anger. If you have tried self-help ways of dealing with your anger and if you have a history of anger getting the best of you, then it is worth the time and money to seek professional help. Would you agree anything is better than prison?

Just to emphasize again, there are many books available on how to deal with anger. You can find some in your local library, bookstores, and online if you have access to the Internet. In addition, the books of James and Proverbs in the Bible have some good advice for daily living.

Remember the three questions:

Will your word or actions be good for:

1. You?
2. Another person?
3. Society?

The choice is yours.

Dealing with Anger

Points to Ponder

STOP! Before you deal with the next Key reflect on the following questions:

1. When have you felt anger?

2. What makes you angry?

3. How can you better deal with anger?

Chapter 5

Dealing with Loneliness

It is strange to be known universally and yet to be so lonely

–Albert Einstein

The following is a brief account of a young divorced mother while serving time in a federal prison. Can you identify the mix of emotions she is experiencing—loneliness, fear, and love—all at the same time?

Aug. 29

I talked to my son. He seems to be doing OK. That's the hardest part. I really miss my little boy. I'm afraid he'll get comfortable with his dad.

Sep. 24

I miss my son so much, I miss being a mom. I want to wake him up in the morning and yell at him because he won't get out of bed. I miss those little things.

Breaking Out of Your Prison

Oct. 14

After a visit with my parents and son, I had a hard time when they left. Seeing him reminded me how much I miss him. I love that little boy so much. He just makes me smile and want to be home to be his mom.

June 28

I miss my son so bad. At times I just feel like he is drifting away from me. That really hurts. At breakfast this morning I couldn't stop crying. I really need to see him soon.

Just prior to being released from prison to a half-way house she writes:

Oct. 8

I do feel good about myself. I lost 50 lbs. I can't wait to be able to spend time with my son again. I want to cradle with him at least I hope. I am down to 22 days and a wake up. I'm really getting excited and nervous to leave. I am so ready to get this over. I want my life back.

Get her life back she did. Even though she is still making restitution for her crime she has a good relationship with her son and enjoys a successful business of her own.

***

"I have no one to talk to. I feel so alone. I have been on my own since I was five years old," said one prisoner to me. These

Dealing with Loneliness

are common comments I have heard from those doing prison time. Loneliness is a terrible thing to experience. Doing time in prison can be a lonely time.

If you have a family member, friend, volunteer, pastor, or someone visiting you in prison, be sure to express your thanks. If you are one who has few or no visitors, there are usually many programs for your benefit.

I know organizations like Prison Fellowship, Good News Jail & Prison Ministry, Yokefellow Prison Ministry provide various services both in and beyond prison. These are good for you, if for no other reason, it gets you out of your cell and gets your mind off self. Too much of self is not good for anyone.

And if you are not in a physical prison cell, the same applies. Get out of the house and take advantage of community or church events. Getting out gets your mind off self and how lonely you feel. I'll say again, too much of self is not good for anyone.

Loneliness is a feeling that everyone experiences. It doesn't matter if you are little-known or well-known. Mother Teresa said, "The most terrible poverty is loneliness and the feeling of being unloved."

One observation I have made is that in our current world with all the technology and social networking, people feel the need to be in communication with someone. It doesn't matter if it is in the grocery story, a super store, gas station, restaurant, going for a walk, or wherever, people are talking on the phone, texting, or using other forms of communication. There was a song years ago "People need People," and I agree!

Loneliness is real and it affects us all. It says in the Bible, *"It is not good that man should be alone"* (Genesis 2:18). God knew about loneliness and so He created a woman as a companion for the man He had created. It is normal that we are attracted to one another. It has been said, the character, or mark, of a person is revealed by what a person does when no one else is watching. Being alone or feeling lonely can cause us to think thoughts that are not good. If these thoughts linger in our minds, they can be destructive to our mental, emotional, physical, and spiritual health.

This is where plans to do harm to self or others start. If we are upset, angry, or feel revengeful toward someone, we will try to justify our emotions in our loneliness. So when you feel lonely, do something positive. It may be to exercise, read a good book, or attend a learning or educational program.

Many prisons offer opportunities for prisoners to earn their GED (General Education Diploma) equivalent to a high school diploma. If you have a high school diploma, there are often other educational and job skills training, especially in

Dealing with Loneliness

state and federal correctional facilities. Most prisons have a list of things prisoners can do while incarcerated. A staff member, counselor, or chaplain can inform you of opportunities that can help you with whatever are your needs or interests.

Many times prisoners said to me, "I am just doing my time." You can just do your time, or use the time in a way that will help you. If you make no attempt to help yourself while in prison, most of the time you won't do well after you get out. I know men and women who used their time in prison wisely, and now they are productive citizens of society. Several have their own business; many are employed full time in meaningful employment. One has worked with troubled teens for more than 25 years. He is helping others avoid making the same mistakes he did.

Whatever your experience, lack of family or support, don't let your past keep you there. Use your time to change your future. You can't always do it by yourself. That is why there are many people and programs to help you, but no one can do it for you. You must care enough about yourself to take advantage of the opportunities available to you. Most are familiar with the phrase, "If it's going to be, it's up to me."

Loneliness can be a terrible feeling, but don't let it grow into hopelessness. When a person feels lonely and he or she doesn't do anything about it, the feeling can turn into hopelessness.

Breaking Out of Your Prison

When you feel there is no hope for you, it is easy to stop making efforts to help yourself.

Each day you fail to take a step forward out of loneliness, it can lead you toward fear. Often it is a fear of failure. So loneliness, hopelessness, and fear all go together. I doubt you remember your first step as a young child. And I doubt you remember all the times you fell when you were first learning to walk.

Even after children fall a few times, they still get back up and try again. Why do they try again—why did you try again all though it may be years ago—because others encouraged them and they found it gave them a new freedom. So I encourage you to take a new step forward, try something new today, take a small step. You may fall a few times and it may take learning some new skills, but you will reap the benefits in the future.

Rather than concentrating on your loneliness, your time alone can be changed from unproductive to productive if you use your time wisely. Prison in a cell or prison in your bedroom at home can start you on a new future if you learn from it. Talk to someone today about using your time for your own or someone else's benefit. You will be glad you did. Remember the expression, "A mind is a terrible thing to waste," Well, time is also a terrible thing to waste, so use your time as an education for the future, don't waste your time in loneliness.

Dealing with Loneliness

The prisoners whose experiences I have shared with you have all used their time wisely. They often mentioned their appreciation of books sent to them. Most prisons will permit books to be sent directly from publishers. Reading can go a long way toward helping you through the prison experience or other times of loneliness.

Breaking Out of Your Prison

Points to Ponder

STOP! Before dealing with the next Key reflect on the following questions:

1. When have you felt lonely?

2. What caused your loneliness?

3. How are you handling your loneliness?

Key 6

Dealing with Plea Bargaining

Persuade your neighbors to compromise whenever you can.

–Abraham Lincoln

John (not his real name) was a frequent "visitor" to our prison. He was tall, handsome, and soft spoken. He read and knew the Bible well and attended Bible studies, church services, and spiritual programs regularly. John was a likable individual and had many friends. His problem was, when he wasn't in prison, on the "outside," most of his friends used drugs, which led him to steal and rob, which brought him back to prison again and again.

John was seen as sincere about his faith in prison, but when he was released, back to the old crowd he went. He told me many times, "I know the Lord, but I just can't be strong enough to resist the temptation on the streets." Does that sound familiar?

Breaking Out of Your Prison

John would make promises to God, others, and me that this time he was going to go straight. Every time he would return to prison many of the staff would say, "Chaplain, your buddy is back." This behavior is what is often referred to as "jailhouse religion."

How many times have people said, "Lord, get me out of this mess and I will become a believer! Heal me of my disease and I will honor you with my life. Lord, bring my lover back to me and I will follow you the rest of my life." Surveys and experience have shown that most of these promises are empty.

When the prisoner is released, when the sickness is cured or put into remission, and the lover returns, the biggest percentage of people never honor those promises to God and return to their former lifestyles.

There is no question that "bargaining" is a stage we go through when we find ourselves in a hole that seems beyond our reach. It is also a step in handling the emotions of incarceration—real or self-inflicted.

After people get through the initial emotions of denial (I can't believe this is happening to me), they usually get angry with themselves, others, or God. That is when they start bargaining with their legal advisers, parole, or probation officer. It is at this stage when people want to make some kind of deal to better the situation. It is human nature. They may ask their

Dealing with Plea Bargaining

public defender, attorney, or legal counsel to do everything they can to get them the best deal. In legal terms this is called plea bargaining, but more about that later.

I need to relate a real life story. If you know anything about yard sales or garage sales, the prospective buyer often starts a bargaining process. If the interested person sees something he would like to buy, he may ask the seller if he would take less for the item, and may make an offer. Often the seller may make a counteroffer. With that in mind, here is my story.

Recently a grandfather took his granddaughter to a yard sale where a tent was being sold. The grandfather told the granddaughter, a teenager; "Don't be afraid to make an offer if it is more than you want to pay." She was not too sure she wanted to do that. When she got to the yard sale, she asked the cost of the tent. The wife of the couple having the sale said thirty dollars. The husband standing nearby asked, "Why do you want the tent?" The granddaughter said, "I want to take it to 'Creation' next year." The wife said, "You can have it for twenty dollars." The husband quickly said, "If you want it to go to 'Creation', you can have it for ten." Granddaughter happy. Deal done? Not quite!

Now for the reader who doesn't know, "Creation" is a four-day annual Christian music festival with special speakers held on a large farm in Central Pennsylvania. People of all ages attend and camp out. It is especially popular with young people. Now the rest of the story.

As the grandfather and granddaughter were loading the tent into their van, the wife came up to the granddaughter and said, "Here, you can have these two cots also…and here is your ten dollars. My husband and I agreed we just want you to have the tent. Enjoy it and have a good time at Creation." The granddaughter was so excited and came home and wrote the couple a beautiful "Thank you" note. I saw the whole transaction because I was the proud grandfather.

That is bargaining when the result went all one way. The buyer walked away with a free tent and the seller had nothing. It was certainly a better deal than the buyer ever dreamed of making. No one would question that my granddaughter got the best bargain. Even after she had already agreed to a price, she was offered even a better deal. She already knew when to say yes to the deal at ten dollars. The key is to know when you have a deal.

Unfortunately, we often bargain with God and don't realize when He is offering us the very best deal ever made.

There is a story in the Gospel of Luke that tells about the time when Jesus called Zacchaeus to come down out of a sycamore tree so Jesus could go to his house. Zacchaeus came down and said, "Look, Lord, I give half of my goods to the poor; and if I have taken anything from anyone by false accusation, I restore fourfold" (Luke 19:8).

Dealing with Plea Bargaining

We often bargain with God, our parents, teachers, and employers for various things. To a parent we may say," Let me have the car tonight, and I will mow the lawn for you tomorrow." To the teacher we may ask, "What can I do to get a higher grade?" To the employer we may plead, "Don't fire me for being late, I promise to be on time from now on." To our attorney we say, "What can you do for me to get a lighter sentence?" Your lawyer may ask you, "What are you willing to confess to?" That is bargaining. In the criminal justice system it is often referred to as plea bargaining.

***

What exactly is plea bargaining? A successful plea bargain is when an agreement is reached between the prosecutor and defendant. In this agreement the defendant agrees to plead guilty without a trial; and in return, the prosecutor agrees to dismiss certain charges or make favorable sentence recommendations to the court. Plea bargaining is expressly authorized in statutes and in court rules.

While there may be differences of opinion by many about the plea bargaining process, proponents of plea bargaining contend that both defendants and society reap benefits. Defendants benefit because both the defendant and prosecutor help to fashion an appropriate punishment. Society benefits because it is spared the cost of lengthy trials while defendants admit to crimes and still receive punishment.

Breaking Out of Your Prison

You may remember earlier in the section on denial I related that often I would have inmates say to me, "I think I can beat the charges" meaning the charges can't be proven. When I was asked what to do, I would tell them, "Confess or plead guilty to what you are guilty of—no more, no less." That was often not what they wanted to hear.

When there are multiple charges, this is when plea bargaining can leave many options for the defendant. It is important to remember it is the prosecutor who has the discretion whether to offer a plea bargain. As a defendant, you have to recognize when you have a deal. It is the key to bargaining, just as in the tent story. What you are dealing with is much more serious than whether you are going to camp out for a few days in a tent. It is about weighing what you have to barter with and how long you are going to camp out in prison.

May I suggest that whatever your plea bargaining result is, don't look at it as a punishment but as a bargain (which the word means) or a prize. Yes, my granddaughter got a bargain, she didn't pay what she expected to pay, she didn't deserve it, but the owner was generous. So look at your plea-bargaining as a bargain compared to what it could have been.

Do you realize that we as human beings got a bargain when Jesus went to the cross for our sins? We didn't deserve it because the Bible says, *"all have sinned and fall short of the glory of God"* (Romans 3:23). It also reminds us *"while we*

Dealing with Plea Bargaining

were still sinners, Christ died for us" (Romans 5:8). *That* is a bargain! Don't complain about what you got—be grateful for what you didn't get.

Do you know the difference between justice, mercy and grace? Justice is getting what we deserve, mercy is not getting what we deserve, and grace is getting what we don't deserve. I believe plea bargaining is in there somewhere. What do you think?

Breaking Out of Your Prison

Points to Ponder

STOP! Before dealing with the next Key reflect on the following questions:

1. When have you bargained with someone that resulted in benefits for both?

2. What did the bargaining process include?

3. What did you learn about the bargaining process that can help you in the future?

Key 7

Dealing with Fears

Don't let the fear of striking out hold you back.
—Babe Ruth

When I entered the ministry as a second career, believe me it was frightening. I was married with a family and home mortgage. I left a secure job with the United States Postal Service. I was required to get a college degree and after that attend seminary. That took eight long years to complete. During that time I was assigned to a rural church as a pastor.

Many times I experienced fear. I feared I would not be able to handle the course load at college and adjust to a completely different schedule. I feared that I would not be able to meet my mortgage payments. I feared that I might not be able to handle the busy duties of a minister of the church. Most of all I feared I would fail as a husband and father to my two young daughters.

Breaking Out of Your Prison

Many times I would wonder how I was going to make it. But I did make it, thanks to a very supportive wife and family and church congregation. It took work, discipline, prayer, and faith.

***

What is your greatest fear today? Fear doesn't only happen to the incarcerated. Most people who experience something new or different experience a degree of fear. For example, a person moving to a new community, starting a new job, or a student leaving home for the first time to attend college can be filled with fear. Even new relationships can be a little frightening.

In other words, anything new can make a person become fearful. Partly because we don't always know what will be expected of us, which presents the possibility of failure—and who wants to fail. Fear of failure is a common human emotion.

Bill Cosby, the great comedian, said, "In order to succeed, your desire for success should be greater than your fear of failure."

And former U.S. President Franklin D. Roosevelt said, "The only thing we have to fear is fear itself."

The Bible tells us that, *"God has not given us a spirit of fear, but of power and of love and of a sound mind"* (2 Timothy 1:7).

Dealing with Fears

It is always good to know that when we are going through a difficult time, that we are not the only ones who have experienced it. The question is, what can we do about our fears?

As we deal with different emotions, whether within or beyond prison walls, we will experience fear of one kind or another. The best way to handle your fears is to face them. I know many people who put off for years what they wanted to pursue because their fears were greater than their desire or lacked the faith to pursue their dream.

For years I have had book writing on my bucket list, as they say. Finally as I sat down to write this book, I ask myself the same questions I have asked you many times:

Is it going to help me? Yes. Because it has helped me discover afresh how many emotions we face whether in or out of prison.

Is it going to help others? It is certainly meant to do so. I write for no other reason than to bring hope, joy, meaning, and faith to prisoners, families, all who are affected by the criminal justice system, and all those who have imprisoned themselves.

Third, Is it going to help society? I know the advice and insights I write will help society if each reader applies it to his or her life. If it helps one person break out of the prison of emotions and prevents him or her from returning to prison, then it was worth it. If it helps people in general to better understand

Breaking Out of Your Prison

themselves or prisoners and their emotions, then this book will have answered my basic questions with a "YES!"

As you consider your fears, they will be different from mine, but overcoming them will be every bit as rewarding. The self-satisfaction of knowing you put the effort, time, and resources into conquering your fears can change your life forever.

I encourage you today to take the first step to overcoming your fears. Seek out the right people and do your research and step forward, which is the hardest part. It is easy to sit around and complain or say "if only" or feel sorry for yourself; but remember, God did not give you a spirit of fear, but rather a spirit of power of love and a sound mind. You *can* overcome your fears!

Dealing with Fears

Points to Ponder

STOP! Before you deal with the next Key reflect on the following questions:

1. When have you felt fear?

2. What caused your fear?

3. What steps do you need to take to overcome your fears?

Key 8

Dealing with Depression

Recession is when your neighbor loses his job, depression is when you lose yours.
—President Ronald Reagan

"I am so depressed, Chaplain, what can I do?" Those were the words of an inmate who asked to see me. As we talked, I asked him, "What are you doing with your time?" He said he was doing some reading. I asked him what he was reading.

"Well, I have been reading some books on the occult and Satanism," he said.

"So what are you thinking about when you are reading those books?" I asked.

"Well, I'm thinking about what I am reading," was his reply.

"So do you think your depression has anything to do with what you are reading?" I asked.

Breaking Out of Your Prison

"Well I guess it could," he said.

I then tried to find out what interest he had in sports, auto mechanics, or learning new job skills. I suggested he read more positive books such as *The Power of Positive Thinking* or the Bible. I suggested he give some of these types of books a try and see if it helped his depression. He said he would try. I also suggested other books about how prisoners dealt with their prison experience to overcome depression.

Several weeks later we talked about how he was doing. "Much better," he said. He changed his reading habits and was in a much better frame of mind. In the coming weeks we talked about how what we put in our minds can affect our personality, thoughts, words, and actions. We discussed how different things can cause us to feel negative about ourselves, others, and life in general.

It is not only what we put into our minds from books, movies, television, and the like, but unexpected experiences can also cause depression. Examples include: receiving a bad doctor's report, ending a close relationship, experiencing the death of a loved one from a sudden accident or illness, losing a job, or being confined in a prison cell can all be depressing. Depression comes in different ways.

Remember we said earlier that when an unexpected event happens, often our first reaction is denial in the form of "I

Dealing with Depression

can't believe it." We then become angry, which can lead to fear or depression. It doesn't matter how or what the crisis is, we are seldom emotionally prepared for the effects it has on our lives.

Everyone can have feelings of discouragement and hopelessness, which can lead to depression. If these feelings are not faced in the early stages, they can lead to long-term depression. Some people experience depression for a lifetime.

***

What can you do about depression? We already talked about changing what we put into our minds. I know for me, watching the news on television can become depressing. So when I get tired of hearing so many bad things on the news, I turn it off or walk away. I often ask myself and others, "If I didn't watch television, listen to the radio, or read the newspaper, would I have a more negative or positive outlook on life?" The reply is always "more positive."

Many counselors and professionals have suggested that much of depression is caused by being too self-centered. If you are a person who is always thinking about self and how important you are or have little contact with others, it is easy to get down on yourself.

Breaking Out of Your Prison

One thing that can help overcome depression is to do something nice for someone else. It may be just a nice word, phone call, or letter to a friend. Let me be quick to say, I realize in prison good deeds to the wrong person can come back to haunt you later in the form of expected favors which may not be legal or moral. It is a sad fact of human nature, but we need to be "wise as serpents and harmless as doves," In other words be cautious.

Another suggestion is when you have the opportunity, become involved in something bigger than yourself. This can be in a volunteer program or projects within or outside the prison setting. Look for something to occupy your time in a positive way.

As I study and teach the scriptures, one author continues to amaze me. Apostle Paul wrote thirteen books of the New Testament—he wrote four of them while he was in prison! When you are depressed, I suggest you read the book of Philippians. Here Paul was in prison for preaching the Gospel, and he was writing to believers to think about what was honorable, true, and pleasing. In other words, look at the good things happening around you—don't dwell on the bad things. As the saying goes, "Is your glass half full or half empty?"

Whether you are a believer or not, you can learn something from Paul. You may have heard the expression that what we are in a year from now will depend on the books we read and the

Dealing with Depression

friends we make. If we want to change our lives, we have to do some things differently. We can't do things the same way and expect different results.

The exercise at the end of this section will help you measure how you are doing with depression. You can do it more than once to measure your progress. It may not be something you deal with one time and it is gone. Keeping yourself busy will help you greatly.

Points to Ponder

STOP! Before you deal with the next Key reflect on the following questions:

1. When have you felt depressed?

2. What caused your depression?

3. How can you better handle your depression?

Key 9

Dealing with Reality

When we are no longer able to change a situation, we are challenged to change ourselves.

–Victor Frankl

Bill (not his real name) is an ex-prisoner for years doing well in his own business. The following is only part of his story:

I was in trouble before, drinking, smoking dope, stealing. I never got caught. But sooner or later you are going to do something wrong and get caught. That is what happened to me. I got caught with thirteen charges of burglary. There were many more after that. The worst of all I was charged for stealing from my own parents. I spent many years in prison, both county and state.

I always wanted to be a winner. I know there is only one who can help you change your life, and this one is the Lord Jesus Christ. My prayer is that you will allow Jesus to come into your heart and give you the peace that I have found.

I can confirm this testimony, which is much longer. No doubt he has changed.

There does come a time when we need to deal with the realities of life. We must sooner or later come to grips with our situation and make the best of it. Even though you still may be experiencing some of the emotions already discussed, how do you deal with the reality of what is?

You may still be trying to work a deal with your attorney or other people in the criminal justice system to receive as light a sentence as possible. It could be that you have reached a plea bargain agreement. Maybe you are happy with it or unhappy about the results. Nevertheless, you may be getting to the point where you are beginning to question yourself about where you go from here.

It is always the unknown that can cause much uncertainty. But once you have made a decision about the amount of guilt you are or are not willing to confess, it has or will affect your future plans, whether in a local, state, or federal prison facility. That decision may have come from a plea bargain or through a trial in the courts of law. If you're fortunate enough to receive parole or probation, it will also involve some decisions for your future beyond prison walls. Any of these outcomes will require you to make some choices about yourself.

Dealing with Reality

As you plan for life beyond where you are now, consider what Albert Einstein said, "Learn from yesterday, live for today, hope for tomorrow."

Anyone who has been through a crisis realizes they have to make some adjustments. If you have experienced the death of a close family member or friend, frequently it forces some changes in living arrangements, finances, and other issues. If you have lost a meaningful relationship through divorce or separation, you have experienced similar adjustments. Life is full of adjustments to new situations.

Your involvement with the criminal justice system is no different. So the question is, as you come to realize the reality of your situation, what can you and what are you willing to do to move on to make the best of your situation? Remember we said earlier that it doesn't matter what happens to us that makes a difference but *how we respond* to what happens to us.

So in facing your situation, what are you learning? Where do you need to start to make yourself over? The first two issues to consider: 1) what are you doing in your spare time? This is true in or out of prison. So consider what are you putting into your mind through books, videos, movies, etc., and 2) who are you hanging out with? Remember what was said earlier, what we put into our minds and who we hang out with will determine our future.

Breaking Out of Your Prison

To learn from the past requires us to look back. Ask yourself:

- Who are my friends? Did they have anything to do with my charges and imprisonment? If so, do you want to go back and hang out with them?
- If your charges had anything to do directly or indirectly with drugs or alcohol, are you going back with the same group? You may say but they're my friends. I ask you, are they doing your time for you? Do you love them more than you hate prison?

That is why often the next thing you need to do is make new friends. That is not always easy but it is possible. That is part of your makeover in becoming a new person.

Another important step to take that can help you cope and give you a new start in life is your education. Work on your education or job skills. If you don't have a high school education, work on earning that. It is called a GED (General Education Diploma). This is available in most prison facilities and community programs. If you have your high school diploma and need further education to pursue a career or job, check out prison or local resources. If you have access to the Internet, you may be able to take courses online.

If education or job skills training is not available in your situation or if you have no need or desire to consider that, often the correctional facility has duties to perform for pay or volunteer.

Dealing with Reality

If you are on probation or parole or are in your personal prison and struggling to get free, check to see what work or volunteer needs there may be in your community.

Be aware, depending on your charges or situation there may be limits on what you are permitted to do. If you know anyone who has a business, they may be willing to give you an opportunity. I have known many employers over the years who are willing to give people on work release a chance—if they can see you making an effort to change yourself.

Making yourself over isn't an easy thing. But unless you are willing to work on yourself, the criminal justice system could become too familiar to you in the future.

Another thing you can do, whether in or out of prison, is improve yourself by taking educational courses, vocational training, or applying for volunteer work. You can increase your knowledge by becoming a frequent visitor to the library in prison or a local library in your community. Through reading and learning you can become a better candidate for employment. These steps can help you gain self-confidence and are excellent ways of meeting new people who can open opportunities for social and employment opportunities.

Attend as many programs as possible in prison and beyond, be they social, educational, or spiritual. All of these are ways to face your situation and improve it. All these opportunities

Breaking Out of Your Prison

can change your thinking, which is a good start to a personal makeover.

Apostle Paul said, *"do not be conformed to this world, but be transformed by the renewing of your mind..."* (Romans 12:2). Norman Vincent Peale said, "Change your thoughts and you change your world."

These are the first steps in facing the facts and becoming a new person. You are on your way!

Dealing with Reality

Points to Ponder

STOP! Before dealing with the next Key reflect on the following questions:

1. When have you dealt with the facts and tried to make some changes in your life?

2. What did you do and how did it go?

3. What are the facts and changes you are willing to work on now?

Key 10

Dealing with Acceptance

Success is not final, failure is not fatal: it is the courage to continue that counts.

–Winston Churchill

Have you ever received a gift on a special occasion, such as Christmas or your birthday that you weren't happy with? You may have thought or said, "That isn't what I wanted, that isn't what was on my list or what I asked for." That same thing can happen in the court system, whether it is plea bargaining or through a court trial. You may not get the sentence you were wishing for, but you have two choices—accept it or appeal it.

If you decide to appeal, be ready for a long and costly process. If you accept the sentence, the question is: how will you accept it or how are you accepting it?

Acceptance is often the final stage in dealing with any crisis in our lives. This was confirmed in patients struggling with the

Breaking Out of Your Prison

dying process. They often come to the point of accepting their situation, knowing they can't do anything more about it. Even though they may say such things as: "What's the use," or "I just can't fight it any longer," it is not a resigned and hopeless "giving up." They often mean it is the beginning of the end of the struggle. It does not always mean that "acceptance" is a happy stage.

In the United States it seems we have interpreted the words, "Life, liberty, and the pursuit of happiness" to mean if I am not happy 100 percent of the time, I am not living to my fullest. Anyone familiar with Rick Warren's book, *The Purpose Driven Life* knows that his opening statement is, "It's not about you." If that is where our life is centered—on us—then we need a new purpose.

I am not suggesting it is wrong to be happy or that we need to walk around with long faces all the time. I am simply suggesting that we have life struggles and life is not just one big party. If you are always planning a party, at a party, or coming from a party, are you facing the truth and realities of life? I think not.

I know many people, as I am sure you do, who have prolonged health problems. Many of them deal daily and hourly with pain and discomfort. We know people who were born with abnormal limbs or without them. The list could go on. Their diagnose is only somewhat treatable not curable. Are they happy about it? Of course not, but few of them complain and let it control what they *can* do. Many of them continue to work or do volunteer work in their community, hospital, church, and in many other ways.

Dealing with Acceptance

Life does sometimes hand us things that we didn't expect or ask for, but we must deal with it, accept it, and move on. Sometimes it is because of some bad choices we make that we pay a price. One of the Bible verses that comes to mind is Galatians 6:7, *"We reap what we sow."* That is why I have said several times in this book in different ways, be careful what you put into your head and who your friends are.

Has the time come for you to accept your situation and get on with your life? You can accept your situation, sentencing, and all that goes with it and get on with your life. You may not be happy about it. But it may be the right time to say "OK, I am ready to accept my situation and make some choices." It is a good time to ask:

Is what I'm about to do going to help me?

Is it going to help another person?

Is it going to help society?

Remember, you are the only one who can change you. We can all play the blame game, but it ultimately comes down to you taking responsibility for your actions.

The great basketball player Michael Jordon said, "If you accept the expectations of others, especially negative ones, then you never will change the outcome." People may be down on you or you may just think they are. You may think that others don't care about you, but how much do you care about

Breaking Out of Your Prison

hardships or pain your actions may have caused others? You can change that.

Earlier I referred to a question I asked in a chapel service about how many people were affected by their being in prison. The average response was seven. So you may have more people than you know who want the best for you and mean the world to you.

I ran across a phrase that I think is so true: *To the world you may only be someone—but to someone, you may be the world!* Think about it. Who is your world to you? Who do you mean the world to? Is that person worth dealing positively with your situation and moving on? Yes! Take your time, whatever it may be that you need to change or do, and plan now to try some of the things mentioned before.

Remember, accepting your situation does not always mean you are happy with the way things turned out, but by accepting the situation and doing whatever you can to be positive will bring happiness to you and your loved ones.

Whether you think your sentence is just or you feel like a loser, it is the courage to continue that counts. Once you accept your circumstances, you will have the courage to continue. Acceptance can be an ongoing gift for you and your loved ones.

***

One of the things I often hear is, "But how can God love me after what I have done? Once I get my life straightened out,

Dealing with Acceptance

then I will do so and so." I ask them, "Do you go to a doctor when your well? Do you take your car to a mechanic when it is working?" I found out real quick in life that I was not a mechanic. When I tried to fix my car, I only made it worse.

That is the way it is with our lives, when we try to do it all ourselves, we often make it worse. We go to the doctor when we are sick; we take our vehicle to the garage when it is not working. Most people, especially over the age of 18, learn to trust in God during a crisis in their lives. We get it all backward. Rather we need to place ourselves in God's hands before a crisis and He will give us the courage to face whatever comes our way.

It is discovering the truth of Ephesians 2:8-9, *"For by grace you have been saved through faith, and that not of yourselves; it is the gift of God, not of works, lest anyone should boast."* This is the whole concept of forgiveness. We come to God as we are: broken, sick, in a crisis and battered. We try to handle life on our own, thinking we are strong; we don't need anyone's help. But after we mess up our lives God's says, *"Come to Me, all you who labor and are heavy laden, and I will give you rest"* (Matthew 11:28).

When you know God accepts you as you are, then you have a new focus, which gives you courage to accept the truth about yourself and move on with your life. Are you going to keep doing things your way or are you ready to accept God's forgiveness of the past and move on? What is holding you back?

Breaking Out of Your Prison

Points to Ponder

STOP! Before dealing with the next Key reflect on the following questions:

1. When have you had trouble accepting a difficult situation in your life?

2. How did you deal with the situation?

3. What are you struggling with accepting now?

Chapter 11

Dealing with Temptation

May we think of freedom, not as the right to do as we please but as the opportunity to do what is right.
—Peter Marshall

Jim was having trouble with a female relationship. He felt cheated on and unloved. He was upset, in fact, downright mad, using some very strong language. Besides that, he was having trouble with some of the guards. He vented his feelings as I listened to him. I attempted to calm him down, made some suggestions, and before he left my office, we had prayer together.

I reminded him when something doesn't go his way, walk away, exercise if possible, or write down his feelings. Sleep on it overnight. In the morning re-read it, tear it up, and destroy it. Forgive, forget, and move on. It isn't easy, but if anger and bitterness are left to eat at you, there will be more damage done

Breaking Out of Your Prison

to you than the other person. For when you hold a grudge or a get-even attitude, you let the other person control you. It limits your freedom to enjoy life. Jim finally came to terms with the situation.

Dealing with our various emotions is an ongoing battle. You and I will deal with many emotions over and over during our lifetimes. The key is not only recognizing them but also knowing how to handle them when you have to deal with them again.

Depending on where you are in your physical or emotional prison experience, you will be taking on more individual responsibility. With responsibility comes freedom, be it in or out of prison.

If you are doing time, long or short, the way you handle your emotions will directly affect how you get along with other prisoners and staff. So be careful with your emotions when something doesn't go your way.

How you handle your emotions can affect your release date as well as your freedom upon release. Remember, with freedom comes responsibility. You have been used to having to obey prison rules, including mealtime, showers, etc. Someone else has set the schedule. You have had someone else tell you what and when to do something. The Apostle Paul tells us, *"Do not use liberty* [freedom] *as an opportunity for the flesh* [self-indulgence]" (Galatians 5:13).

Dealing with Temptation

Freedom does not mean do as you please, it means to do what is right to remain free. That is not always easy. It is not always hard to do the wrong thing, and it is not always easy to do the right thing—but it is always worth the effort to do right.

The story goes that there was a man walking down the street one day swinging his arms. As he passed a man walking in the other direction, his arms hit the man in the nose. To which the man responded, "Hey, what do you think you're doing?" The one doing the hitting said, "It's a free world, isn't it?" The one hit said, "Yes, but where my nose begins…your freedom ends!" The point is, our freedom requires responsibility, which requires respecting the rights of others.

As you learn more and more to enjoy your freedom, it will require more decisions that will cause you to ask these questions many times:

Will my decision be good for me?

Will it be good for the person I love or who loves me?

Will it be good for society?

If you can answer a definite yes to those three questions, then continue cautiously. If not, then rethink your words or actions. That is when you may need to talk to a trusted friend, counselor, chaplain, or spiritual adviser. Never feel it is wrong, weak, or childish to seek advice from someone who can look more objectively at your situation. It is part of being free.

Breaking Out of Your Prison

One thing we have not talked about until this point is temptation. Again, it is one of those emotions that affects every one of us almost daily. It is not always easy to walk away from temptation, especially if it is a behavior that has been part of the past. After being released, it is too easy to meet up with old friends and return to old habits. It could be habits or behaviors that were partly or wholly responsible for you being in prison in the first place.

A perfect example of this is when I would discuss a home plan with inmates before their release. When talking about where they were going to live and with whom, I would always ask if anyone in the household used drugs or alcohol. If they said "yes," and that was a problem related to incarceration or forbidden as a condition of parole, I would ask, "How are you going to handle that?"

Often their answer was, "Oh, I'm not going to use them." To which I would say, "Do I look like I was born yesterday? Who do you think you are fooling? Do you really think you are strong enough to live around that day in and day out and not eventually submit to the temptation?"

Do you know the Lord's Prayer says, "lead us not into temptation"? Why do you want to put yourself right in the middle of temptation? It is like an alcoholic wanting to stop drinking but goes to the bar every night, or someone wanting to give up sweets but goes out and buys a pound of chocolate. If you have

Dealing with Temptation

trouble with gambling and you want to stop—don't visit the casino every night.

Let me be quick to say, I know we can't always remove ourselves from every temptation, but don't flirt with it either. Paul says in First Corinthians 10:13: *"No temptation has overtaken you except such as is common to man; but God is faithful, who will not allow you to be tempted beyond what you are able, but with the temptation **will also make the way of escape**, that you may be able to bear it."*

When the temptation comes, put on your running shoes and take off!

Temptations come in all forms, from stealing something that you really want to eating too much. Temptation comes from our flesh, especially regarding sexual sins. Jesus says, *"The spirit is indeed willing, but the flesh is weak"* (Matthew 26:41). How powerful temptation can be! The poet Henry Ward Beecher said, "All men are tempted. There is no man that lives that can't be broken, provided it is the right temptation, put in the right spot." That is why you need a strong group of people who can give you encouragement and support to help you from submitting to temptations and help you find freedom to make the right decisions.

A meaningful faith can set you free: *"So if the Son sets you free, you will be free indeed"* (John 8:36 NIV). You will have the freedom and the courage to keep emotions in check so that

Breaking Out of Your Prison

you make *decisions that are best for you, best for the ones you love, and best for society.*

As you overcome one temptation, it will strengthen you for the next one. Don't yield to temptation, yield to Christ and you will be given strength to walk away from temptation rather than allow yourself be drawn into it.

Dealing with Temptation

Points to Ponder

STOP! Before dealing with the next Key reflect on the following questions:

1. When have you experienced temptation and had the courage and freedom to walk away?

2. What was the result of that experience?

3. As you recall that event, do you see how it gave you strength to handle the next one that came along?

Chapter 12

Dealing with the Future

For I know the thoughts I have toward you, says the Lord, thoughts of peace and not of evil, to give you a future and a hope (Jeremiah 29:11).

Are you one of those guys who are feeling down, depressed, or blue five days a week? And have the 50/50 look at life, always nervous and impatient wondering if you will get back out in the world and mess up again. Or maybe you are one of those guys who rely on your so-called friends to help make your decisions. Well why don't you try starting over, and come and talk with the Chaplain, and learn a little about the Lord. You know as well as I do, that it doesn't hurt to try. You tried cigs, drugs, alcohol, and criminal actions. Why not give the Lord a chance. I think he will change your life. I know it won't be easy at first, but when you start to feel comfortable, and will be able to talk freely, you will begin to feel good on

Breaking Out of Your Prison

the inside. You will be moving step by step into a whole new world, without drugs and all of those nasty habits you picked up as a kid. Give it your best shot. Just remember it don't hurt to try.

Written by Charles on his own. Here was a young man searching for new meaning and hope in his life. This was one among many who would share with me about the change faith has made in their lives.

You might say talk is cheap. I could not agree more. It is so much easier to speak about our faith than to live it out. I will let you in on a little secret. Do you know what really confirms that a person has changed? It is when another inmate or staff member says, "Wow, he or she has really changed!" If our faith is real, it will show in our words and actions.

Remember, none of us are perfect. There will always be those who will test us. As I talked to prisoners they would often say, "Well I am trying, but I still do this or that." Many times they would be struggling with bad language or curse words (the 3-4 letter kind). I would tell them, "Don't be so hard on yourself. Ask yourself, *'Are you doing it less than last month or last year?'* Bad habits are not easy to break. That is why you need a support group to encourage you."

Again this is a reminder of the need to be aware of what you are putting into your head and the friends you hang around with. For example, if you want to quit smoking and your partner

Dealing with the Future

has no desire to quit, it's going to be much more difficult to stop smoking if you spend time with that person or people who smoke. That's a fact.

It has often been said that you can face anything as long as you don't have to face it alone. Consider that truth as you reflect on the verse at the beginning of this chapter. God wants the best for you. Choose the friends who want the best for you and you will experience new hope for your future.

Hope can be a motivating force in your life. Just as a student looks forward to graduation, a bride-to-be looks forward to her wedding, a prisoner looks forward to his or her release. Having something to look forward to gives you hope because it is something positive that changes your attitude. Hope motivates your faith. Faith and hope go together like pie and ice cream. We live by faith today in the hope of tomorrow. Faith is for today, hope is for tomorrow.

Many times I would hear a prisoner say, "I'm going to give up _____" (you fill in the blank). Giving up bad habits is a great step in the right direction! But if you don't fill that now-empty "blank" with something good and positive—like reading the Bible or good books, doing something nice for someone, educating yourself, etc.—then that blank will get filled up with temptations or negative thoughts or emotions.

When many people are asked how they are, they reply, "I'm surviving." We were not put on this earth just to survive. Jesus

Breaking Out of Your Prison

said, *"I have come that they* [you] *may have life, and that they* [you] *may have it more abundantly"* (John 10:10). Who doesn't want that? Everyone wants an exciting, abundant, full life that brings meaning and hope. That is what I have attempted to bring to you in the pages of this book. You are a person with unique talents, abilities, and gifts that can bring life to you and others. You may have made some mistakes, but you don't have to keep making the mistakes that bring you back to prison. With Jesus, you can set yourself totally free—and stay free.

The following is a summary of things that will give you hope for the future:

1. Keep educating yourself or learning new skills. Use your local library or services in your community. Think seriously about your strengths and then improve them. Maybe you are good with your hands, you are creative, you like to work outside, or maybe you have a good mind for numbers or words. Whatever gift you have, focus on it and then seek training to make it marketable.

2. Find someone—an agency, professional person or volunteer—who can help you in preparing a resume (life's education and work record). Then submit your resume for jobs that interest you—places where you can use your skills.

3. Don't hide and become a loner. Seek trustworthy advice from someone who has your best interests at heart.

Dealing with the Future

The best way to get better at anything you do is to work at it with someone who has more experience than you. That is true throughout life. That is what an apprentice and a mentor is all about, someone who works or walks alongside you to help you with new trades, skills, and goals.

4. Don't forget a spiritual mentor! Whether you have taken a new step of faith in prison, or even while reading this book, don't depart from wherever you may be in your journey of faith. Follow through. Keep or seek whatever spiritual contacts or mentors you discovered while in or out of prison. They are keys to your well-being, hope, and goals as you continue to discover the plans God has for you. God has hopes for you, and so do I. What are your hopes?

5. Think positively and be hopeful your future will be brighter than your past. Pray daily for strength, courage, and trust in the Lord. He hears your every prayer.

***

Breaking out of your prison does not mean allowing your emotions to run wild and doing as you please; it means controlling your emotions to do what is good for you, other people, and society. Being released from your physical prison is minor compared to being released from your emotional prison. If you apply these principles to your life as others have, you too can

Breaking Out of Your Prison

break out of your emotional prison and discover a new life of freedom.

What is keeping you from breaking out of your emotional prison? Define it, and then do whatever it takes to destroy it so you can lead the abundant life that you were meant to live!

Dealing with the Future

Points to Ponder

As you complete this book, reflect on these questions:

1. When did you experience a time of hope in your life?

2. What was the lasting hope of that event?

3. What are your current hopes for the future?

Remember the three basic questions to ask yourself during a crisis or before making a decision:

1. Is what I am about to do going to be good for me?
2. Is what I am about to do going to be good for another person?
3. Is what I am about to do going to be good for society or glorify God?

I encourage you to read the true story of hope in the following Conclusion that was written by a volunteer after one of her visits to prison.

Conclusion

A volunteer wrote the following story. My prayer is the Spirit of God will touch your life as it touched her life and others during a service at our local prison.

The Melting Heart of a Prisoner

On a beautiful spring morning as the birds were singing and the sun was shining through the clouds, it was my first day to sing at the Franklin County Prison.

It was a day of happiness, excitement, and wonder of the adventure God had in store for me. Carolyn, our pianist at the Marion United Methodist Church, asked me to go with her to sing at the prison. Without hesitation I said yes.

We drove to the prison, proceeded to turn over our belongings, and entered with just our music to glorify God. Passing through the different areas and hearing the prison gates slam behind us was a real jolt. It made shivers run down my spine thinking about being in there for any length of time. But I had no fear.

Breaking Out of Your Prison

We were escorted to the chapel. The chaplain was there to greet us and thanked us for coming. After the inmates were seated, the service began as Carolyn played the piano. We sang and prayed. The song I chose to sing was "Pass It On," words and music by Kurt Kaiser. Here are the words:

It only takes a spark to get a fire going,
And soon all those around can warm in it glowing;
That's how it is with God's love, once you've experienced it;
You spread His love to everyone, you want to pass it on.

What a wondrous time is spring when all the trees are budding,
The birds begin to sing, the flowers start their blooming,
That's how it is with God's love, once you've experienced it,
You want to sing, it's fresh like spring, and you want to pass it on.

I wish for you my friend, this happiness that I've found,
You can depend on Him, it matters not where you're bound:
I'll shout it from the mountaintop; I want my world to know:
The Lord of love has come to me, I want to pass it on.

Conclusion

After I sang, the highlight and blessing of the day were yet to come.

After the sermon the chaplain asked for prayer requests. A young man, probably in his early 20s, asked if we would pray for his 4-year-old daughter, who was having heart surgery the next day.

What happened next was heart-wrenching. The man was surrounded by everyone in the chapel who then placed their hands on him while the chaplain prayed one of the most moving prayers I have ever heard. The chaplain lifted up the little girl, her family, and the care of doctors to the loving hands of our Lord and Savior Jesus Christ.

Needless to say there was not a dry eye in the whole room. What an emotional experience, God was definitely in prison with us.

Joy came a few days later when Carolyn called, after hearing from Chaplain Ray, and told me the little girl's heart operation was a success.

God has an unconventional way of sometimes touching our hearts in the most unusual places. It is an experience I will never forget.

I have been fortunate to cross paths with Chaplain Ray several times after this wonderful experience. I am proud to say

Breaking Out of Your Prison

Ray and his wife, Georgia, are special friends and blessings in my life.

Blessed to be a volunteer,
Phyllis

***

I trust this book has brought some meaning and hope to you and especially those who have experienced incarceration at any level of the criminal justice system.

There are many kinds of prisons, but there is only one Truth. You *can* break out of your prison—the prison within is easy to escape when you allow Jesus to fill your body, mind, and soul with His never-ending love and forgiveness.

About the Author

Ray L. Kauffman is an ordained elder of the Susquehanna Conference of the United Methodist Church. He has served as a church pastor, prison chaplain, chaplain to migrant farm workers, and nursing home chaplain. In his retirement he continues to be an active volunteer in many community endeavors. He is married with two daughters and three grandchildren. He and his wife, Georgia, live in Chambersburg, Pennsylvania.

Contact Ray
Ray L. Kauffman
395 Lincoln Way East
Chambersburg PA 17201